"This is a practical handbook for the bereaved and their friends; how to live with grief, to express it or not, how to find your *natural* way through. The quotations from Neruda, Machado, Dickinson and others are beautifully chosen."

—Coleman Barks, translator of *The Essential Rumi*

"This is a book that every person should own, read and reread. It is filled with practical suggestions concerning how to help people grieving the death of a friend or relative. Every page rings true."

—Patton Boyle, Episcopal priest, pastoral counselor, author of *Screaming Hawk*

"This book tenderly touches every pain-swollen corner of a broken heart. This conversation incarnates the healing presence of God's grace...a gentle washing of the soul with hope, a telling of truth that restores the breath of faith."

—Reverend Helen W. Appelberg, Founder of Compassionate Friends

"(This book) is sensitive, insightful, and practical to anyone who finds themselves wondering what to say, what to do, and what not to do in regards to a grieving friend or family member."

—Marina Maimer RN, St. Louis MS Hospice

"This tenderly written book speaks to the heart of the process of accompanying loved ones through loss and bereavement. It is a much needed addition to an area rarely addressed in the literature dealing with grief and loss."

—Chris Ingenito, L.C.S.W., Hospice Care of Sonoma County

SUPPORTING THE BEREAVED IN UNPRECEDENTED TIMES

AS MUCH TIME AS IT TAKES (SERIES)

MARTIN KEOGH

INTIMATELY ROOTED BOOKS

**Supporting the Bereaved
in Unprecedented Times
AS MUCH TIME AS IT TAKES (Series)**

Poem by Thomas Carlisle entitled "Our Jeopardy" © 1987 Theology Today. Originally published in issue 43 (1987): 559. Reprinted with the publisher's permission. Adapted by Jack Kornfield.

Excerpts from Gratefulness, the Heart of Prayer: An Approach to Life in Fullness by Brother David Steindl-Rast. Copyright © 1984 by David Steindl-Rast, Paulist Press, Inc. Used with permission of Paulist press. www.paulistpress.com

The poems by Antonio Machado are translated by Robert Bly. Used with permission of the translator. (Times Alone. Middletown, Conn.: Wesleyan University Press, 1983)

Excerpt from "It Happened in Winter" from Extravagaria by Pablo Neruda, translated by Alastair Reid. Translation copyright © 1974 by Alastair Reid. Reprinted by permission of Farrar, Straus and Giroux, LLC.

- ISBN hardcover:
- ISBN paperback: 978-1-9990208-8-0
- ISBN ebook: 978-1-9990208-7-3
- ISBN audio book:
- ISBN large print:

Intimately Rooted Books
Salt Spring Island, BC Canada
martinkeogh.com

DEDICATION

The friend who can be silent with us in a moment of despair or confusion, who can stay with us in an hour of grief or bereavement, who can tolerate not knowing, not curing, not healing and face with us the reality of our powerlessness, that is a friend who cares.

–Henri Nouwen, *Out of Solitude*

CONTENTS

INTRODUCTION

We live in the unprecedented time of a pandemic. This has led far too many of us to bear the sudden loss of a loved one.

The skills and rapport needed to support the bereaved are rarely taught in school or by our families. Yet each of us may be called on to have these abilities, sometimes when we least expect it.

Like perhaps, now.

If you wish to reach out to someone who has lost a loved one or companion during this outbreak this book is filled with practical and heartfelt ways to offer your support.

If you yourself are bereaved, this book can help you appreciate and articulate your feelings and needs during this difficult and perhaps overwhelming time.

Supporting the Bereaved is filled with guidance that not

only applies to loss from Covid-19, but all the causes of death arising as our healthcare system becomes overwhelmed. You will find tools in this book that apply to all these losses.

This guide arose in response to the particular challenge of offering and receiving support when there are restrictions on travel and proximity. How do we proceed when it may be not be possible to enter our friend's home to cook them a meal, to help with our physical presence, or to offer a hug?

This book is written in the voice of the bereaved. When you turn the page and begin reading, these are the words your bereaved friend might be having trouble saying. Or if you have lost someone yourself, this book might help you to understand and give voice to your needs and emotions.

You can read this book in under an hour, yet my hope is the abilities and skills you gather here will help you deepen your relationships for a lifetime.

PROLOGUE

My Dear Friend,

I HAVE SOME TERRIBLE NEWS.

SOMEBODY I CHERISH HAS JUST DIED from the outbreak. I'm going through a challenging time right now, and I could use your support.

I REALIZE that sometimes it's hard to know how to help someone who's grieving. One day we need company and the next day we need time alone. Sometimes, all we need is a friendly ear and sometimes the reminder to eat.

YOU MIGHT BE afraid to do or say something that can cause me distress. It's sometimes challenging and confusing to know when and how to help. So, I've drawn this roadmap for my friends. With all that's happened, it's difficult to ask for support. That's why I'm giving you this little guide.

NOTHING in here takes a huge effort. I certainly don't want you to do anything that doesn't come from your love for me. In truth, most of the time, all I need is the small reminder that you care.

ON THE FOLLOWING PAGES, you will find many suggestions. Select the ones that feel right for you. You might be comfortable helping with practical matters, such as coordinating paperwork and obtaining the death certificate. Or you might wish to lend me an ear and give emotional support. This book is designed to help you discover what kinds of support are the most natural and genuine for you to offer.

YOU'LL ALSO FIND activities and clichés to avoid. Your sensitivity to this information will encourage my healing.

WITH DEATH SO CLOSE, each moment has become more precious. I'm grieving now, but I do want you to know I care for you. Thank you for being in my life and for all you've given.

With deep gratitude...

I

IT SEEMS IMPOSSIBLE

FIRST AID FOR THE RECENTLY BEREAVED

I sat in the garden,
spattered by the great drops of winter,
and it seemed to me impossible
that beneath all that sadness,
that crumbled solitude,
the roots were still at work
with no one to encourage them.

–Pablo Neruda
(Translated by Alastair Reid)

1

I've just learned of the death of my loved one.
   I don't want to be treated like someone
   who's infirm or bedridden.
   But sometimes, the smallest tasks
   feel overwhelming right now.

YOU MIGHT ASK: *Is there anything I can do?*

IN THIS STATE, I'm often not sure
   what I want or need.
   If I'm unable to answer you –
   and this is likely –
   please offer something specific.

I want to help you understand
　　what I'm going through.

Sometimes, it's overwhelming for me
　　to live with this much emotion
　　(or numbness).

You don't need to get overwhelmed as well.
　　As you read the suggestions in these chapters,
　　please remember you don't have to do
　　everything.

These are choices.
If you're so moved,
select what feels natural for you.
These are the kindnesses
I'll appreciate most.

3

I'm emotionally exhausted.
   Sometimes, I'm forgetful.
   My mind may be foggy.
   Small details seem overwhelming.

TELL me this is natural
   for someone who has just suffered
   this kind of loss.

4

Healing from an emotional injury
    is similar
    to mending
    from a physical injury.

ENCOURAGE me to get enough rest and sleep.
    Ask if I have eaten today.
    (unless you see me suppressing
    my feelings by binge eating).

Feel free to drop off food,
    especially homemade food
    that only needs to be heated and served.

ASK me if there is something I'm craving.
    Ask what food I loved growing up or
    if I have special dietary needs.

I MIGHT FIND comfort foods most appealing. Find out if my comfort foods are creamy, salty, bland, spicy or crunchy.

OR GET my friends together here: takethemameal.com

6

I'm having trouble
   telling people about my loss.
   On top of my own tidal waves
   of emotion (or numbness),
   I have to deal with
   other people's reactions
   and discomfort.

YOU COULD HELP
   by offering to send emails
   or make phone calls
   so I don't need to be the first
   to tell people the news.

7

There are so many ways
   to be together virtually.

IN REALTIME we can use the phone,
   messenger, Skype, Zoom or Whatsapp.

OR WE CAN CONNECT ASYNCHRONOUSLY with
   Voxer or Marco Polo.

IF IT WORKS FOR YOU,
   tell me I can get in touch with you anytime –
   day or night.

8

Sometimes, you might find me angry,
    especially because the pandemic
    has caused me to endure a sudden loss.

- I'll rage at the disease
- Call the doctors "incompetent buffoons"
- Blame you or myself for not "flattening the curve"
- Lash out at my friends who "don't understand"

If you can, stay with me and
let me feel my anger. This too will pass.

If I have children,
    offer to spend time with them
    virtually or if possible, in person.
    I might need someone responsible
    to take care of them,
    until I am better able to function.
    I may need to rest and grieve alone,
    knowing my children
    are in safe hands.

BUT PLEASE UNDERSTAND,
    if one of my children has died,
    I might not want anybody else
    to take care of my surviving children
    for a while.

See if I've taken care of business.
    Ask me if I've paid my utility bills
    or if I have any other pressing
    financial obligations to handle.
    Have I let them know at work
    that I'm not available?

FIND out if I'm overwhelmed by the
    legal and financial matters of the estate.

Do I have appointments
    that need to be changed or canceled?
    You might offer to handle
    some of my paperwork
    or return phone calls.

If you live nearby, perhaps you could offer to help with:

- Shopping for groceries
- Walking the dog
- Doing the laundry
- Getting me to appointments

If finances are a struggle, you could offer to set up a GoFundMe.

I can feel overwhelmed
    by having to take care of so many details.
    If you're skillful at making arrangements,
    you might offer to help
    with some of these tasks:

- Arranging for the death certificate
- Making plans with the cemetery for the cremation or burial
- Setting up a memorial web page
- Inviting people to a virtual memorial
- Helping to greet people and keeping a list of all who attend or call
- Helping me with correspondence and thank you notes

The pandemic has kept us from gathering in person for funerals and memorials. I might be saddened that these times deprive us of the solace that comes from gathering in community to mark this passing.

YOU MIGHT OFFER to help host an online event. (I might need someone to help with the technology.)

MARKING this passage by a memorial
    or an online tribute to celebrate the
    person's life can be an important part
    of the grieving process.
    It allows me to more fully realize
    that the person is gone
    and gives me the opportunity
    to say good-bye.

Please respect whether I have
    religious or spiritual traditions
    and those of family and friends
    during the memorial
    and the mourning period.

If I am at a loss
for ideas for an online service,
you could gently suggest we:

- Encourage people to share stories about the deceased
- Read letters from friends and family
- Include telling jokes and tenderly "roasting" the person
- Sing their favorite songs
- Share videos, audios, personal mementos, letters, and photographs

II

A FRAGILE CUP OF
REVELATION

Our Jeopardy

It is good to use best china
the most genuine goblets
the oldest lace tablecloth.
There's a risk, of course,
every time you use anything
or anyone shares an inmost moment,
or a fragile cup of revelation.
But not to touch, not to handle,
the artifacts of being human –
is the quiet crash, the deadly catastrophe
where nothing is enjoyed or broken
or spilled or spoken,
or stained, or mended –
where nothing is ever lived, loved,
laughed over, wept over,

where nothing is ever lost,
or found.

–Thomas Carlisle

16

Sometimes, I might feel embarrassed that I'm grieving and so vulnerable. I might become bewildered, not knowing how much I can reveal to you.

SOMETIMES, *you* might feel awkward, not knowing how to communicate with me while I'm grieving.

SOMETIMES IT'S GOING to feel downright clumsy for both of us.

AND THAT'S OK.

Often it feels
as though we need
a license
to make mistakes.

This grants
(insert your name:)

_____

a bona fide license to
feel awkward
or uncomfortable
while in the unfamiliar territory
of the bereaved.

This license gives you permission
simply to be present
to the best of your ability.

III

AS MUCH TIME AS IT TAKES

*The heart is a leisurely muscle. It differs from all
other muscles. How many push-ups can you
make before the muscles in your arms and
stomach get so tired that you have to stop?
But your heart muscle goes on working for as
long as you live. It does not get tired, because
there is a phase of rest built into every single
heartbeat. Our physical heart works
leisurely.*

*And when we speak of the heart in a wider sense,
the idea that life-giving leisure lies at the
very center is implied. Never to lose sight of
that central place of leisure in our life would
keep us youthful. Seen in this light, leisure is
not a privilege but a virtue. Leisure is not the
privilege of a few who can afford to take*

time, but the virtue of all who are willing to
give time to what takes time – to give as
much time as a task rightly takes.

–Brother David Steindl-Rast

In my grandparents' day,
 there was more support for grieving.
 Many generations of the family
 gathered together.
 People wore black for a time
 after a person's death.
 Often, there were wakes and shivas in the home.
 Now, I'm expected back to work right away.
 People expect me to be "fully functional."

THE SMALL REMINDER that I'm grieving
 and may need to slow down
 and heal goes a long way.
 Encourage me to go at my own pace.
 Keep reminding me of the importance of
 putting my own needs before
 other people's expectations.

Encourage me
    not to make
    any big decisions
    for a while.

A big enough
    life change
    has already
    taken place.

I have so much going on inside
    that when you're with me
    virtually or in person
    you don't need to do much.
I probably feel most comfortable
when you give off a calm,
relaxed air that encourages me to feel that:

- There's plenty of time
- There's no rush
- I can take the space I need to feel what needs to
  be felt

When we're together, even on a screen,
make it easy for yourself.
Most times, you don't have to *do* anything.
Just your presence makes me feel better.

If it seems I'm keeping myself
    unusually busy...
    If you see me running around
    most of the time...
    If I'm numb...
    If I'm having trouble crying...
    Invite me
    to spend a lazy afternoon or evening
    where I don't do much.
    Suggest I run a bath,
    or listen to some sad
    or melancholic music.*

*SOME PEOPLE who have suffered a big loss may discover a sudden appreciation for country, blues or mariachi music.

2 3

If it's OK to get together in person,
   come and hang out in my home –
   maybe not even in the same room.

WE CAN SIT AND READ.
   Cook a meal.
   Talk by candlelight.

NOTHING SPECIAL.

AND BECAUSE THIS pandemic has led to so much virtual time, while we are together, let's keep the screens and phones off.

If I live with people, at times
    I may simply need
    the house to myself
    or an afternoon to walk alone
    in the woods.

HELP me preserve
    some intervals for solitude.

ENCOURAGE me
    to put aside time
    in my calendar
    for dates with myself.

Encourage me to get out into nature.
    The simplicity and beauty of nature
    can help bring comfort
    and take me to that deep
    wordless place
    where I can see my loss
    from a broader perspective.

INVITE ME TO:
    • Simply go for a walk outside
    • Get up to a place with a view
    • Watch a sunset
    • Stroll on a beach or sit and listen to a stream
    • Lie down and gaze at the Milky Way

Please don't try to cheer me up
        or save me
        from my feelings.
        By truly going through
        all the feelings that arise
        with losing a loved one
        I'm being brought more deeply
        into my life.
        I'm also being asked
        to look squarely
        into the face
        of my own death.

From a spiritual point of view,
   this can be an important
   time for me.

GENTLY ENCOURAGE me
   to take my time
   with every aspect
   of this process
   and
   to live each stage fully.

IV

A GENTLE AND
TENDER HAND

*When we honestly ask ourselves which person in
our lives means the most to us, we often find
that it is those who, instead of giving much
advice, solutions, or cures, have chosen rather
to share our pain and touch our wounds with
a gentle and tender hand.*

–Henri Nouwen, *Out of Solitude*

I might feel reserved and insecure
    when we first connect.
    I may not be sure of your intentions.

PLEASE TRY NOT to arrive
    with some big plan.
    The first important step for me
    is to establish an unafraid,
    heartfelt communication.

Look for my cues; let me lead.
    I may not know what I want,
    but I'm quickly aware
    of what I don't want;
    please look for signs of my resistance
    and respect them.

WHEN YOU MAKE AN OFFER,
    always give me the option
    of something else,
    or of nothing at all.

SOME DAYS, I don't want to *do* anything.

If you're having trouble
  picking up my cues, try this:
  Take a moment and imagine yourself
  in my place.

IMAGINE you've had this sudden loss
  and what you might be feeling.
  Imagine what you might need
  from those around you.
  You may find you simply desire
  love and acceptance.

In your own way,
    tell me that you love me.
    And why.

TALK to me
    about my strengths.
    Remind me
    of my good qualities.

Send me messages, texts
      or emails. Better yet, send something
      tangible like cards or flowers.
      Remind me that you care.
      Write me a love letter.
      Tell me what you remember
      about the person who has died.

SOMETIMES, it's just too much
      effort for me to reach out to anyone.
      Call me periodically and leave
      simple messages.
      (say it's ok to not respond).
      If you feel like you're
      reaching out too much, ask me.

Find out when it's hardest for me.
Quite likely,
it is Saturday evenings
or Sundays.

INVITE A CONNECTION.
Ask me what I'd like to do
and if I'd like anyone else to join us
virtually or if it's possible, in person.

3 4

With so much going on,
    I might be forgetting my body.
    Encourage me to get exercise.

VIRTUALLY OR IN person
    join me in some quiet stretching
    to bring me *home*.
    Or join me in some activities
    that get my body moving,
    my blood pumping,
    and my sweat flowing.

If we can get together safely in person,
    offer to massage my feet
    or hands.
    Rub my shoulders.
    Ask if I would like a full massage.

OR LET'S sit on the couch
    with our feet touching.

My sex drive might drop
    for a while.
    Or it may go up.
    If we have a sexual relationship,
    please be sensitive.

OPENING up sexually
    at this time
    may make me feel especially vulnerable.
    I may cry when we make love.
    And these tears may be just what I need.

Help me to surround myself
   with beauty.

SUPPORT me in keeping my personal
   environment peaceful and harmonious.

- Ask me what colors I feel good wearing
- Fill my kitchen with flowers
- Remind me of the music I like

Create a ritual with me.

It can be simple. Online or together we can:

- Light a candle by the deceased's photo
- Sing their favorite songs
- Tell stories of when they were most sweet, courageous, maddening or funny
- Write, draw, or dance our feelings about this loss
- Chant, pray, or meditate together
- Call out their name

You're giving a lot to me right now.
Please remember: *Take care of yourself.*

KNOW YOUR LIMITS.
Don't overextend yourself.
If you're deeply uncomfortable
around tears or anger, let me know this
and excuse yourself when I cry or rage.

Take time away when you need it –
in the next room, in nature,
or any way that works best for you.

V

GIVING SORROW WORDS

Give sorrow words; the grief that does not speak
Whispers the o'er-fraught heart, and bids it
    break.

—William Shakespeare

I'm trying to understand
    what has come crashing
    into my life.
    By wrapping words
    around my experience
    and my feelings,
    I'm attempting to make sense
    of a life that is
    now vastly different.

MAY I TALK TO YOU?

CAN I tell you my stories?

I don't know how to describe
what's going on inside me.
But I may need to try.
And it will take a while.

ASK ME,
"How are you doing *today*?"
when you genuinely have the
time and receptivity
to hear the answer.

Sometimes I might get stuck
    trying to be "appropriate"
    or trying to please you.
    As we talk, it helps me
    when I feel there's nowhere else
    in the world you'd rather be.

REMIND me that I don't need
    to entertain you
    or take care of you.
    And if you can,
    listen to what I say
    with a calm and open silence.

If it's safe for us
    to be together,
    place yourself
    sitting, standing,
    or lying down,
    at the same level
    as I am.
    Let your body be open,
    your arms and legs
    uncrossed.
    Let yourself be relaxed.
    Don't be afraid
    of eye contact
    (and don't force it).
    If it feels right,
    ask if you can touch me.

It helps if you use little cues
    to let me know you're listening.

WORDS, phrases and questions like:

- Really?
- Mm, uh-huh, and oh!
- How did that make you feel?
- That's awful...
- What happened next?

These tell me
you're listening
and interested.

Questions that call for "yes" or "no" answers can make me uncomfortable:

- Were you happy together?
- Are you hurting?
- Were you satisfied with the memorial?

Because once I've answered "yes" or "no,"
I often don't know what to say next.

INSTEAD, use open-ended phrases and questions like:

- How did you meet...?
- What was it like at the end...?
- Tell me one of your favorite memories...

These encourage me to talk.

Don't pull me out of my feelings
   with small talk.
   I don't need to be distracted
   from my grief right now.

But you also don't need
   to put on an air of false solemnity.
   In fact, sometimes a sense of humor
   is just what's needed.
   Humor used skillfully
   often helps to bring some movement,
   some levity,
   and a deepening of emotion.

On my lead,
    bring in some gallows humor.
    And don't be shocked
    when I make jokes
    about the dead...
    Sometimes,
    the most healing activity
    is to laugh at death.*

---

*A MAN in a bereavement group who had been married for 52 years was about to take his wife's ashes across the border. He was trying to imagine what he would say if a customs official tried to open the urn. "If he sticks his hand in the urn, I'm going to have to tell him, 'Get your hand off my wife's ash!'"

4 8

─────────────

Don't be surprised
    when I surround myself
    with photos of my loved one…
    Or when I wear their shirt to bed…
    Or when I go to the places
    we visited together…
    Or when I do anything else
    that helps bring my memories to life.

Or I might hide everything
    that reminds me of my loss.

Reminisce with me.
  Tell me stories
  about the one I've lost.
  Bring them closer
  by invoking their memory.
  Allow me to tell the stories
  of our relationship –
  of the pleasures and betrayals,
  of our adventures and misadventures.
  And allow me to tell you about the hole
  I feel in my heart.

50

Try not to philosophize
or strive to make me feel better.

THIS DEVALUES my feelings of loss
and makes me feel judged for my pain.

51

Watch out for using expressions like these:

- Everything will be okay
- They will always be with you
- Good thing he's out of pain now
- I'm sure she's looking down on us from heaven now
- You're lucky you had so much time together
- Someday, you'll look back at this and...

When I hear phrases that attempt
to counteract what I'm feeling,
I sometimes get confused or upset.
I'm grieving and the emotions
I'm feeling are part of the healing process.

If I say something like "This sucks," it is not right," you might respond with something that recognizes my state, "Yes, it does suck. It is not fair at all."

. . .

AND RATHER THAN SAYING, "I'm sorry," say something like, "I can't even begin to imagine what you're going through" or "It pains me to see you going through so much loss."

More clichés to avoid:

- You must be strong (for the family/for the children etc.)
- I know she wouldn't want you to cry
- You are not alone—many people have had losses
- At least he didn't suffer for long
- God will never give you more than you can handle
- You should count your blessings (or any other "should")

Please don't try
    to solve my "problems."
    Stay away from giving advice.*
    If I ask you for advice,
    you might first ask me,
    "What do *you* think?"
    Or: "How do *you* feel about it?"
    And please don't preach.

JUST BE BY MY SIDE –
    an equal, a human being, a friend.

---

*IF YOU FEEL COMPELLED to give advice, advise me to accept offers of help from my friends. I'm probably having some difficulty with this.

If we both have lost someone
    to the virus,
    we can be an invaluable resource
    for one another
    during this difficult time.
    Our ears can be wide open
    with compassion.
    Let's allow each other
    to have our own timing
    and individual styles of grieving,
    even though we are suffering
    a similar loss.

55

Don't be afraid
    to speak the name
    of the deceased.

THIS IS WORTH REPEATING:

DON'T BE afraid
    to speak the name
    of the deceased.

Don't feel the need...

to fill...

...the silences.

59

After some silence,
    I might want to say:
    "You're giving me a lot right now."

SOMETIMES I JUST WANT YOU TO know
    I'm extremely grateful
    for your presence.

VI

MY HEART AND THE SEA

Lord, you have ripped away from me what I
loved most.
One more time, O God, hear me cry out inside.
"Your will be done," it was done, and mine not.
My heart and the sea are together, Lord, and
alone.

–Antonio Machado
(Translated by Robert Bly)

Tears are nature's balm
    for emotional injuries.
    Your permission for me to cry
    is one of the most loving things
    you can give me right now.
    If I cry, I'm revealing the confidence
    I have in you.
    I trust you enough
    to show you my vulnerability.
    Remember that I won't cry forever
    (and that crying sometimes
    leads to laughter).

61

It's okay to cry with me.
    However, don't *expect* me to cry.
    Sometimes, my tears are spent,
    or I might be someone
    who doesn't cry around others.
    You might simply hear me sigh
    instead of crying.

IF YOU CAN'T TAKE my tears,
    if they make you too upset
    or confused, let me know.
    We'll work something out.

From moment to moment,
 different voices will rise up in me:

- I didn't appreciate him enough
- I hate her for dying
- If only I had...
- It's all my fault
- It's all their fault
- It should have been me who died
- I'm overwhelmed, it's too much, I'm afraid
- I'll never love again

THESE VOICES ARE ACCOMPANIED
 by strong emotions.
 If I trust you enough to speak them
 in your presence,
 please don't invalidate them.

Don't respond with phrases like:
"Oh no, that's not true; you'll be fine,"
or "You did all you could,"
or "Of course you'll love again."

ACKNOWLEDGE this is
    what I'm feeling at this time.
    Recognize that it must be hard for me,
    rather than telling me
    that what I'm feeling
    is not true
    or that it will be different
    someday soon.

63

Let me have my feelings now.
  Perspective can come later.

I want to tell you
   about our last days together,
   about how we met.
   I want to tell you I feel bad
   that I didn't appreciate him enough
   while he was alive.

I WANT to show you her picture
   and tell you about the plans we had...

...THAT SHE TREATED ME BADLY,
   gave me lots of gifts,
   was unbearably ornery.

I WANT to tell you I feel guilty
   that a part of me is relieved
   he's dead.

. . .

I WANT TO WAIL, WHY?
   Where is she?
   How could this happen?
   How can God do such a thing?
   I want to shout,

NO! IT CAN'T BE TRUE!

If I get emotional
    and the words are not coming easily,
    you can reassure me
    with phrases such as,
    "Take your time."
    "It's okay."

ALLOW me to do most of the talking.
    Feel free to ask questions,
    but have your own responses as well
    so it doesn't become an interrogation.
    Once I open up,
    please don't change the subject.
    If you're getting overwhelmed,
    let me know.

People sometimes say to me,
    "I understand."

THIS CAN MAKE ME ANGRY.
    Not even I can fathom
    the depths of my feelings right now.
    How can anyone else say
    they understand
    what I'm feeling?

IT'S BETTER to say thing like:

- I can't imagine what you're going through...
- I'm here with you...
- Tell me about it...
- It doesn't feel fair...
- I'll stay close by, so you can find me when you are ready...

Hearing my stories might remind you
of your own losses and sorrows.

SHARE THEM.

WHEN I HEAR about similar stories
and feelings,
it helps me to feel like I'm not crazy,
despite all that's going on inside me.

BUT PLEASE BE BRIEF,
so that I don't get pulled out
of my emotions.

If I'm angry,
offer to accompany me
to the railroad tracks,
so that I can scream
as loud as I can
as the train passes by.
Guide me to safely
beating or hollering
into pillows at home.
This expression of my fury
also works by the ocean.
It's big enough
to absorb all my anger.

If you're feeling strong,
    stay with me
    as I curse God
    for the injustice!
    For the loss!
    For this death by virus!
    God doesn't need
    your defense.
    Sometimes, what's felt inside
    has to be said aloud
    (very aloud)
    to be released.

Sometimes, I'm going to be intense,
　　sometimes irrational
　　and sometimes numb.
　　At times, it's not going to be easy
　　to be at my side.

BUT KNOW,
　　I'm glad you're with me
　　as I go through this.
　　I *need* you here.
　　And I appreciate your willingness
　　to be at my side
　　even through the discomfort.

And remember to be sensitive
   to your own feelings.

IF YOU'RE uneasy
      around my anger,
      say, "I'm uncomfortable,"
      rather than trying to distract me
      by changing the subject.

IF YOU FEEL anxiety or fear,
      you don't need to pretend
      it's not there. Tell me.

THIS HONESTY WILL BRING us closer together.

I welcome your feelings...

...BUT PLEASE DON'T GET SO
   emotionally distraught
   that I end up
   jumping out of myself
   to take care of you.

In the end, what you say
  or do is not what's most important.
  Your attempts to open up to me,
  to be with me in a vulnerable,
  sometimes uncomfortable
  and compassionate place in your heart,
  will likely be healing for *both* of us.

IT MIGHT TAKE MORE energy
  than you imagined
  to be with me through these dark days.
  But it can create a deep bond
  of friendship between us.

VII

BONE BY BONE

There is a pain so utter –
It swallows substance up –
Then covers the Abyss with Trance –
So Memory can step.
Around-across-upon it –
As one within a Swoon –
Goes safely – where an open eye –
Would drop Him – Bone by Bone

–Emily Dickinson

People sometimes make
a hierarchy of dying.
They might feel it's better
to die of heart failure than from cancer –
it's better to die of cancer than AIDS –
it's better to die of AIDS than suicide.
Please don't let your judgments
affect your compassion for my loss.

KNOW I have lost someone to the coronavirus.

YOUR SENSITIVITY and ability to be responsive
with my particular loss
are welcome.

There was no time for a proper farewell. I'm crushed I didn't get to say goodbye in person.

THEY WERE TAKEN FROM ME. We parted at the ambulance, or at the hospital doors.

IN A SPLIT second our lives changed forever.

WORST OF ALL, they had to die alone.

If I've lost a child to the virus,
    I'm in a particularly sensitive place.
    We're not made to live through such a loss.
    We're not supposed to bury our children.
    This kind of 'out of order' loss feels
    different than any other.

PLEASE DON'T COMPARE my loss
    to the loss of a parent,
    a spouse,
    or a pet.

Some clichés to avoid
around the death of a child:

- God wanted another flower for his garden
- Well, you still have_____
- At least it was now and not when they were
  older and you were even more attached
- You can still have another child

If you can, be there
    for my children and their grief.
    Just like the time you spend with me,
    listen to my children
    with wide-open ears.
    It's important
    not to use euphemisms
    such as "gone away,"
    "left us," or "is sleeping."
    These can be misinterpreted
    and cause the child anxiety.

LET my children know
    my emotions of grief or anger
    or withdrawal are about
    the person who died.

REASSURE my children

they are not responsible
for my feelings:
"He's not sad because of
anything you did;
he's crying because he's unhappy
that your grandfather died last week."

TOGETHER, you can create
little rituals of good-bye –
draw a picture, write a letter,
or blow out a candle
for the one who has died.

They died, and I survived.

IF YOU FIND me speaking of insomnia, nightmares, or irritability –

if you notice I'm having increased startle response or hyper-vigilance –

if you find me questioning the meaning of life –

if you hear me say things like,

- "It should have been me…"
- "I'm still here and they are gone…"
- "I don't deserve to be here…"

I'm suffering from a common response to this kind of tragedy:

Survivor's guilt

If you find me suffering from survivor's guilt,
  remind me that I've lived through
  a harrowing experience,
  and you care for me,
  and you are relieved I survived.

ACKNOWLEDGE ALL that I'm feeling right now. Let me know these feelings are common in survivors of this kind of catastrophe.*

IF YOU ALSO HAVE LOST SOMEONE AND have similar feelings of guilt, tell me so I know I am not alone.

REMIND me that these were extreme circumstances and that these waves of feelings are part of grieving the loss.

* STUDIES SHOW that as many as 90% of survivors of this kind of event report feelings of guilt.

If you hear me say things like,
    "I'd be better off dead"
    ask me if I'm thinking about suicide.
    If I say "yes," ask me if I have a plan.
    If I say "yes," direct me right away to a:

- Therapist
- Spiritual counselor
- Member of the clergy
- Suicide prevention hotline

If you see me retreating
into excesses of alcohol, drugs,
or time online:
offer similar support.

AND MAKE sure there are people
    to reach out to me and to stay in
    contact at all times.

8 2

If I own a gun
   and you see
   I'm extremely distressed,
   offer to take care of it for a while.

AND TELL me I really am
   important to you
   and that you'd never want to see
   any harm come to me.

Put me in touch with individuals or groups who have survived a similar loss.

You can locate information about bereavement support groups online or through a local hospice or hospital.

If I've lost a child, get in touch with a Compassionate Friends group and have one of their members contact me:
www.compassionatefriends.org

VIII

WATER OF A NEW LIFE

Last night, as I was sleeping,
I dreamt – marvelous error!
that a spring was breaking
out in my heart.
I said: along which secret aqueduct,
Oh water, are you coming to me,
water of a new life
that I have never drunk?

Last night, as I was sleeping,
I dreamt – marvelous error!
that I had a beehive
here inside my heart.
And the golden bees
were making white combs
and sweet honey
from my old failures.

Last night, as I was sleeping,
I dreamt – marvelous error!
that a fiery sun was giving
light inside my heart.
It was fiery because I felt
warmth as from a hearth,
and sun because it gave light
and brought tears to my eyes.

Last night, as I was sleeping,
I dreamt – marvelous error!
that it was God I had here inside my heart.

–Antonio Machado
(Translated by Robert Bly)

Now that some time has passed,
　　now the outbreak is behind us,
　　I have more vitality.
　　I keep noticing signs of life.

THIS DEATH WILL BE a part of me always,
　　but I'm beginning to remember
　　the person with more feelings of love
　　than loss.
　　The world is a more inviting place.
　　I have more energy
　　for giving to others and to you.
　　Life all around me
　　(and in me)
　　is perking up!

There comes a time
    when structure can be helpful.

ENCOURAGE me
    to put some things
    in my schedule.
    Join me hiking, swimming,
    playing sports, or any
    kind of getting out.
    Remind me of activities I enjoy.

GET me involved in some projects –
    especially projects where I get to help others
    who are less fortunate than me.

Bring over animals
    and children
    and plants
    to keep me company
    and to remind me
    of life.

Keep sending cards or emails,
    even when it appears
    that everything is back
    to "normal."

IN TIME you can send greetings
    without referring to the loss.

Please don't assume
    I have finished grieving –
    weeks, months, or even years later.

YOUR SUPPORT and love
    are always welcome...

...HOWEVER, if after a long time,
    my life appears *paralyzed*
    in grieving,
    encourage me
    to work with a counselor
    or a bereavement group.

One of the kindest things
　　you can do is get in touch
　　or spend time with me
　　during and just before and after
　　the hard days:

　　　　• birthdays: theirs and mine
　　　　• holidays
　　　　• the anniversaries of their death

It can still be too easy for me to
    get caught up
    in other people's rhythms and needs.
    You might see people smothering me
    with an excess of well-intentioned kindness.

PLEASE PLAY "INTERFERENCE" for me.
    If some *yakkety-yak* comes up
    and starts overwhelming me
    with chatter,
    come and engage them,
    so I can slip away.

Why don't you and I
    go out and have some fun?
    Invite me to socialize,
    perhaps starting with small groups
    and working up from there.
    Invite me
    to reconnect with old friends
    and meet new people.
    Offer to accompany me
    as I head out into the world again.
    I may need a companion
    for driving to work,
    taking a class,
    spending a few hours
    at the beach or park.

I'm more sensitive and perceptive
   because of the range of emotions
   I've been living with.
   Inside, I'm opened up
   in new and stimulating ways to experience
   people, nature, and the world.

Now that I'm grieving less,
   I have more energy.
   This combination of increased energy
   and heightened sensitivity
   makes this an ideal time for creativity.
   Encourage me to get involved
   in artistic and creative pursuits.
   Join me if you share my interests.

You know it's been a rough road for me.
Sometimes, I've wondered
if I would make it through.
But with your presence,
your help,
and your willingness to listen,
every day I feel a little more alive.

I *AM* MAKING IT THROUGH,
and you deserve a lot of recognition
for your kindness
and generous support.

IX

MY DEAR FRIEND

This guide is almost finished,
    but not quite...
    You get to complete it yourself.

REMEMBER you have a particular way
    you demonstrate your caring.
    Take these suggestions
    as a framework
    and then express yourself
    in the style that's natural for you.

You can trust yourself.

Sometimes, when we're asked to help,
we're called on to expand
how we see ourselves as human beings.
By helping me with this loss,
you might have found
yourself changed.

MY GRATITUDE RUNS deep
for your willingness
to take this risk.

My Dear Friend,
How can I tell you how important
your support has been?

YOU'VE BEEN by my side through an
extremely challenging period. Your caring
and compassion have helped me heal
and grow into living my life more fully.

I WILL NEVER FORGET we've shared
some of the most vulnerable and intimate
times that people can experience together.

THANK YOU.
I want to tell you,
I love you.

AFTERWORD

Dear Reader,

I wrote the original edition of this book as a labor of love after losing both my parents and a best friend in close succession.

Since you've made it this far into the book, I imagine you are in one of two groups. If someone near you has died, from the bottom of my heart, I hope you found some solace in these words. If you are in the supporting position, I hope this has been a helpful resource for deepening your connection.

As this pandemic progresses, there is an expanding circle of people who need this information. This is a sensitive topic. The big three, Facebook, Amazon, and Google are rightfully throttling down any marketing with the words "Covid-19" or "coronavirus" to prevent profiteering. This makes it hard for me to reach the people who urgently could use this book.

It turns out, once again, that the best way to reach folks is by word of mouth. If you found this book helpful, please help me get the word out. You can do this by letting people know how it helped you on social media, by leaving reviews, and sharing it in online bereavement groups.

You can also support a grieving person by gifting them this book. I suggest sending them the print version so they have something to hold.

Thank you for helping. These are unprecedented times where we need each other more than ever.

I send you an embrace from my home on the Salish Sea,

Martin Keogh

P.S. I'm ending this book where it began:

> *The friend who can be silent with us in a*
> *moment of despair or confusion, who can*
> *stay with us in an hour of grief or*
> *bereavement, who can tolerate not knowing,*
> *not curing, not healing and face with us the*
> *reality of our powerlessness, that is a friend*
> *who cares.*

–Henri Nouwen, *Out of Solitude*

ACKNOWLEDGMENTS

This book is dedicated to the memory of my parents, Linda and John Keogh, and to Guillermina Villarreal Sautto (Grillo).

My mother, Linda, was a passionate artist who cherished being the center of attention. She loved to cook, to eat, to create, and to receive praise. My father, John, was a life-long athlete, and a dignified and reserved man. He had a sense of humor that held no punches, and a great fondness for language and leisure. My soul-friend Grillo loved people – and people loved her. She could disarm a bureaucrat, a mean-ass biker, or a close friend with her presence and smile.

I've written this book as a tribute to the vitality and love these three exuded and to the important roles they played in so many people's lives including my own.

My profound appreciation goes to those who were interviewed, and to all who offered feedback on the manuscript. These include hospice workers, grief therapists, priests, midwives, and palliative care nurses.

This book would not exist if it were not for the championing of Kristelle Sim, Elianne Obadia, Mick Diener, and Nina Keogh. They helped give this book its form and poetry.

The following friends had the generosity to not be shy in their feedback: Byron Brown, Cynthia Williams, Deborah Watrous, Dharamkaur Sing Khalsa, Diana Sorus, Donna Brook, Gretchen Spiro, Heather Snow, Jane Baas, Jen Boyak, Jill Cooper, John Davies, John Doyle, John Johnson, Liz Rozner, Lucia Walker, Mary Ford, Megan Lundrigan, Owen Jones, Peggy Dobreer, Rick Wilkes, Robert Bly, Sara Zolbrod, Steve Bryson, Sue Earle, and Tamara Ashley.

For the spark of life, I'm ever grateful to Liza Keogh.

ABOUT THE AUTHOR

 Martin Keogh founded *The Dancing Ground,* an organization that offers conferences and symposia on gender, race, and mythology. He has produced and taught with such notables as Joseph Campbell, Robert Bly, Clarissa Pinkola Estés, Coleman Barks, James Hillman and many others.

After attending Stanford University, Martin hitchhiked 25,000 miles through North America and spent time traveling to monasteries in Japan and Korea. In 1979, he became a Dharma Teacher and director of the Empty Gate Zen Center in Berkeley, California.

Martin was named a Fulbright Senior Specialist for his contribution to the development of the interpersonal partner dance form, Contact Improvisation. For over four decades, he led master classes, teacher conferences, and intensive trainings in 32 countries spanning six continents.

Martin's writings have appeared in nine languages. He is author of Dancing Deeper Still (Intimately Rooted Books, 2018) and the editor of Hope Beneath Our Feet: Restoring

Our Place in the Natural World (North Atlantic Books, 2010).

After the loss of three loved ones in close succession, Martin gathered information from professionals in the bereavement field, including palliative care nurses, hospice workers, priests, and grief therapists. This information was synthesized for the original, As Much Time as it Takes: A Guide to Healthy Grieving (Intimately Rooted Books, 2018).

Martin lives with his family on the shores of the Salish Sea in British Columbia.

www.martinkeogh.com